3.99

The Spur Book of

Map and Compass

Also available:
Knots

The Spur Book of

Map and Compass

Terry Brown and Rob Hunter

Frederick Warne

FREDERICK WARNE

Published by the Penguin Group
Penguin Books Ltd, 27 Wrights Lane, London W8 5TZ, England
Penguin Books USA Inc., 375 Hudson Street, New York, NY 10014, USA
Penguin Books Australia Ltd, Ringwood, Victoria, Australia
Penguin Books Canada Ltd, 10 Alcorn Avenue, Toronto, Ontario, Canada M4V 3B2
Penguin Books (NZ) Ltd, 182-190 Wairau Road, Auckland 10, New Zealand

Penguin Books Ltd Registered Offices: Harmondsworth, Middlesex, England

First published by Spurbooks 1975
Revised edition published by Frederick Warne 1983
7 9 10 8

Contents

Definitions

Bearing: The line between two points, on map or ground, expressed in compass degrees, from 0—360°.

Col (or Saddle): The low land or ridge, connecting two hilltops.

Contour: A line connecting all equal heights on the surface of the ground.

Crest: The highest part of a hill, or range of hills.

Escarpment: The steep hillside formed by a drop in land level, usually at the edge of a plateau.

Left/Right bank: The appropriate bank of a stream or river when facing down stream.

Plateau: A raised plain, usually fairly flat, above the level of the land.

Re-entrant: A shallow valley running into a hill, usually between two spurs.

Saddle: See Col.

Re-section: The process of finding a position by taking bearings on two identifiable points.

Spur: A hill feature, or low ridge, running out from a hill or high ground, often between two re-entrants.

Slopes, Convex and Concave:	A convex slope bulges out in the middle. You cannot see the bottom from the top or vice-versa. A concave slope is the opposite; it 'caves' in, and you can see the top from the bottom (or vice-versa).
Trig point:	A triangular point, marked with a concrete pillar, from which map bearings are made by surveyors.
Vertical interval:	The difference in height between two adjacent contours (usually 50 feet).
Watershed:	The line, usually a mountain range, where waters divide to flow in different directions.

Further definitions will be given in the text of the book.

1

Introduction

Everyone who enjoys, and indulges in, outdoor pursuits or hobbies, as climber, rambler, camper, orienteer or yachtsman, should have, in addition to whatever particular knowledge his own preference requires, a competent grounding in a range of other skills. Among these are map reading, the knowledge of how to use a compass by day and night, of knots and knotting, first aid, camping, survival techniques, swimming, and so on. Some of these may only be useful occasionally, but without them, the outdoor life is not only more risky, but much less fun.

For most, but not all, of these skills, a vast range of informative literature already exists. The aim of this series is to render down this bulk of information into a compact and digestible quantity that can be readily absorbed, and quickly referred to.

Map reading and compass work is no longer the widely known Service-based skill that it once was. Many schools teach it, and some outdoor organizations, such as the Boy Scouts, teach it to their members. Non-joiners, and many people enjoy the outdoor life just because they are non-joiners, have to pick it up as they go along, and hope for the best. Unfortunately this method is self-limiting. A degree of know-how is necessary first, if real knowledge,

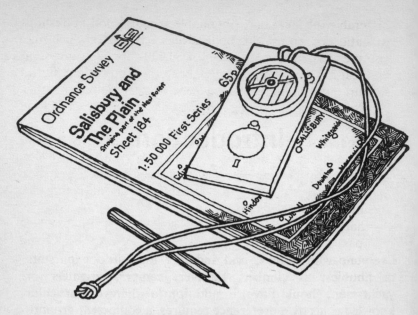

Map and compass—the tools

which usually comes with practice, is to increase, and a
level of reliable competence achieved.

Some Necessary Equipment
We have, in this book, started from zero. We assume
nothing, and we include all that is necessary to walk—or
march, with map and compass—anywhere, at any time,
day or night. The knowledge is here, and on this you can
build.

The skill can only come with practice, and for this a
mountain, while useful, is not necessary. The local. heath,
park or common, a small hill with decent views, or, to begin
with, the dining room table, will be quite sufficient.

Two things **are** necessary and should be purchased
with this book. Firstly, a 1:50,000 Ordnance Survey map,

preferably the local one, obtainable at most good bookshops or stationers. To use this book it does not matter which map you use—provided it is an O.S. 1:50,000—for the same signs and features are common to all. Maps need to be kept out of the dirt and wet. A plastic envelope or sleeve is best for this. Don't invest in a heavy ex-Army map case; they are less than useless.

Secondly, a Silva compass. These cost currently around £10.00 and can be purchased at most camping shops. You can start map reading without a compass, but you will soon want to possess one. If you have difficulty in obtaining one locally, write or telephone Silva (UK) Ltd., P.O. Box 15, Feltham, Middx, TW13 6DF Tel. 081-898 6901. Buy the best compass you can afford and look after it. A sharp pencil and a note-pad are also useful.

Thus equipped we can commence.

The compass points

2
Let's Look at a Map— Information

A map is a birdseye view of a section of ground, on which the roads, hills, houses, forests and so on are represented by lines, colours and symbols.

But before unfolding the O.S. map, look at the information on the cover itself. On the front are listed the area covered, the **sheet number,** the **scale,** and **series,** and of course the price.

On the back of the cover is the index to the Series, shown in map form with the Sheet numbers, and superimposed over an outline of the U.K. Each O.S. map has a Sheet number, and the map Sheets cover the entire country. You need to make a note of the Sheet numbers when ordering maps, and, on a long walk, know which maps you need, East, West, North or South of your original one, so that you have the appropriate map sheet available when you move off the ground covered by the present one. For example, Sheet 128 covers the country around Derby. Sheet 129 to the east covers Nottingham, 119 to the north, Buxton, while to the south, you need either 139 or 140. The back of the cover also gives certain other information, on publication dates for example, for certain scales, and series.

Now let's open the map. If out of doors be careful to do this in a sheltered spot. A gust of wind can rip a map

13

into shreds. Open the map and re-fold it concertina-wise, so that you can unfold it as you progress without having to open out the whole thing again, every time.

The inside cover gives some information on the history and development of the O.S. maps, and is glued on to the top left-hand corner of the map itself. The map has two main parts, the centre coloured section, representing the ground, and a broad margin on the right-hand side, which contains a range of information.

When opening a map, some of the information should be carefully noted:
1. The scale.
2. The date the map was produced or revised.
3. The magnetic variation i.e., the degree by which magnetic north varies from true and grid north, calculated to the map publication date, with the annul change. Note this variation down. You will need it later.

All this can be found in the 'Information' section on the right-hand side of the map. Let's look at these points in more detail.

Scale

Maps are produced to various scales. That is, objects and distances on the ground are reduced in the same proportion, so that the map is, in effect, a scaled down picture of the ground. Some items—probably your house, for example—are too small to appear, and for reasons of scale many things are left out, while others are represented by conventional signs. The information in this book is based on the O.S. 1:50,000 scale, where 2 cm on the map represents 1km on the ground or 1¼" = 1 mile.

O.S. maps are available in other scales, notably the 1:25,000, which the O.S. recommend for walking. Personally, we find the 1:50,000 quite adequate, except perhaps in mountains, where a clear contour definition is useful. For all normal purposes, 1:50,000 is adequate.

The Date

This may seem a small point, but it is nevertheless vital. The date is needed to calculate changes in magnetic variation, and to help you to understand unexpected features you may encounter on the ground. A new housing estate can spring from fertile farmland in two years; equally, buildings and landmarks can disappear. Even in remote regions you may encounter, one dark night, a thick forest on what should be an empty hillside. The Forestry Commission plant conifers four feet high, and they grow a foot a year! If your map is five years old (remember the scale again) the new trees would not be big enough to show when the map was made, and having sprung up since, this sudden forest can be very confusing. So don't panic— remember the date of your map, and changes become understandable. It is also a good idea to buy up-to-date maps.

Magnetic Variation

There are three "Norths".

1. **Grid North:** This lies on the line straight up and down the map and is indicated by vertical **grid** lines.
2. **True North:** This is the north as shown by weathercocks on church steeples and indicates the North Pole.
3. **Magnetic North:** There exists a region in the North of Canada with a strong magnetic attraction. To this spot —called the Magnetic Pole—all compass needles point. The difference between grid north and magnetic north is called the **Magnetic Variation**. The Magnetic Pole is not fixed, but moves a little each year. The annual change can be calculated and is given in the marginal information on all O.S. maps. You need to know the date of the map and the annual change to calculate the correct current magnetic variation. We shall return to this point later, when we are using the compass. Remember that the variation we will use is that between Magnetic North and Grid North.

15

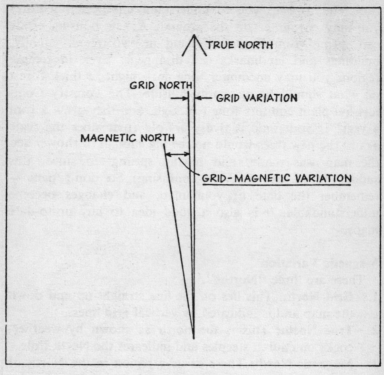

The "Norths"

Now let's look round the edge of the map itself. You will notice, first of all, a series of consecutive blue numbers in line, which appear at the spot where vertical and horizontal lines run off the map. These are the **grid-lines** and the numbers are used for giving **grid references**.

There are also numbers in black, which give the latitude and longitude, with which we need not concern ourselves.

Magnetic North!

Conventional Signs

Down the right-hand edge of the O.S. map is a wide panel which gives the **conventional signs**. These are the symbols, lines or colours used to depict an object, or type of physical feature. These conventional signs need to be learned, which is not difficult and becomes easy with practice. Indeed, they are often drawings of the actual objects and are therefore obvious.

The signs are divided by type. Roads and Paths; Railways; Water Features; Rights of Way; Antiquities; and so on. Spend fifteen minutes studying these signs, then try and find them on the map.

For example:

1. Find a church (a) with spire, (b) with tower, (c) **without either**.
2. Find (a) a railway embankment, (b) a railway cutting.
3. Find a road bridge over a railway and a railway bridge over a road.
4. Assuming you have a map of your own area, trace the road route from where you live to some known point on the map—your work place, favourite pub, kid's school.
5. Identify local features, woods, ponds, golf courses. Draw up a list and find them.
6. Find, (a) a Tumulus, (b) Railway Station, (c) an Orchard, (d) Common, Heath or Downland.
7. Find (a) a Youth Hostel, (b) a Post Office, (c) a call box.
8. Find (a) a spot height, (b) a trig point, (c) a contour value number.
9. Find, and follow on the map, the route of a local footpath.

If you do these exercises, you should acquire a very comprehensive knowledge of conventional signs and the information available on a map, and get some idea of how physical objects are represented. From this point on we can start using the map itself.

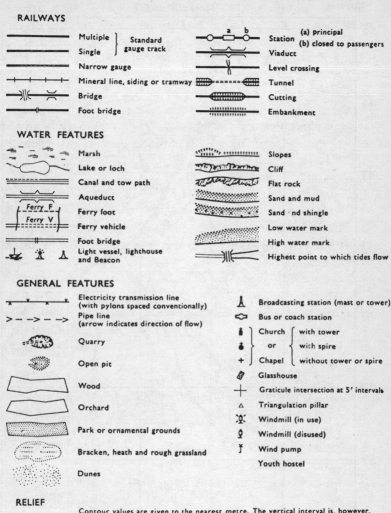

RAILWAYS

Multiple } Standard	Station (a) principal / (b) closed to passengers
Single } gauge track	Viaduct
Narrow gauge	Level crossing
Mineral line, siding or tramway	Tunnel
Bridge	Cutting
Foot bridge	Embankment

WATER FEATURES

Marsh	Slopes
Lake or loch	Cliff
Canal and tow path	Flat rock
Aqueduct	Sand and mud
Ferry foot	Sand and shingle
Ferry vehicle	Low water mark
Foot bridge	High water mark
Light vessel, lighthouse and Beacon	Highest point to which tides flow

GENERAL FEATURES

Electricity transmission line (with pylons spaced conventionally)	Broadcasting station (mast or tower)
Pipe line (arrow indicates direction of flow)	Bus or coach station
Quarry	Church ⎰ with tower
Open pit	or ⎱ with spire
Wood	Chapel without tower or spire
Orchard	Glasshouse
Park or ornamental grounds	Graticule intersection at 5' intervals
Bracken, heath and rough grassland	Triangulation pillar
Dunes	Windmill (in use)
	Windmill (disused)
	Wind pump
	Youth hostel

RELIEF

Contour values are given to the nearest metre. The vertical interval is, however, 50 feet.

.144   Heights are to the nearest metre above mean sea level. Heights shown close to a triangulation pillar refer to the station height at ground level and not necessarily to the summit. Details of the summit height may be obtained from the Ordnance Survey

1 metre = 3·2808 feet   15·24 metres = 50 feet

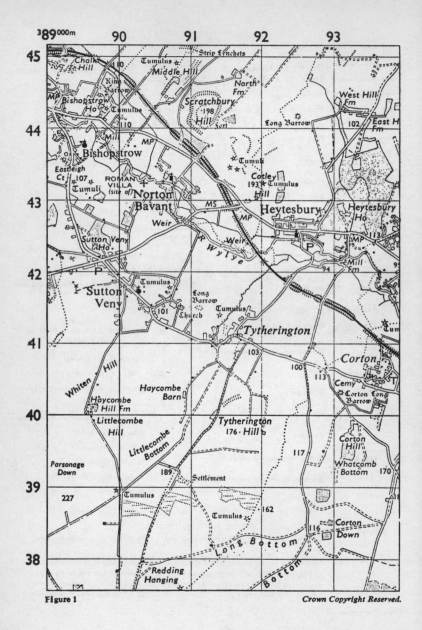

Figure 1

20

3

Let's Look at a Map — the Map Itself

Spread the open map on a table or pin it on a wall, then stand back and look at it from a distance of two or three paces. Try and get an overall impression of the ground it represents. Is it well-wooded or hilly, or threaded with rivers and streams? Are there mountains in the north, and does the land fall away to the south? What is the slope of the ground? What does the map you are looking at represent in physical features? This overall impression of the land will be a great help to you when you are out on the ground.

Before we go out of doors, however, you should know how to find and give a map reference, how to calculate a bearing, and understand a little about contours.

Map or Grid Reference
Both terms are in common use and mean the same thing. We shall refer here to Map Reference or M.R's. M.R's are usually given in six-figure numbers, representing the grid square, and a particular point within that square.

As we have already noticed, the map is criss-crossed with vertical and horizontal grid lines. Each line is identified by a two-figure number, and these give you the first of the numbers of each M.R.—two vertical numbers and two horizontal numbers.

The vertical lines are known as "eastings", for although they run, individually, up and down the map, they **advance** in series across the map from left to right, or heading from west to east—hence "eastings".

The same applies to the horizontal lines which advance in series up the map, from south to north, and are called "northings".

Where two lines intersect you have a grid point, and you can express this by giving the numbers of the grid lines to indicate the bottom left-hand corner of the relevant grid square. Then, to find the point you require within the square, you divide the "easting" and "northing" lines into ten, and pinpoint the spot by referring to the intersection of the imaginary lines which would cut it. With practice you can get these tenths estimated very easily. Otherwise, to be more accurate, you can use the millimetre scale on your Silva compass. Each side of the grid square means 20mm, so 2mm is 1/10 of the line. Try it and see. You can also make yourself a "roamer", or purchase a plastic one of the right scale in a sports shop.

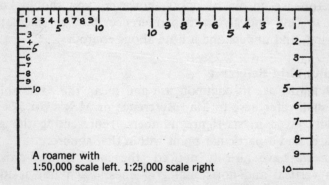

A roamer with
1:50,000 scale left. 1:25,000 scale right

A roamer

22

This sounds complicated, but is in fact quite simple. The point to remember is to give the map reference in the **correct order**. The correct order is to give the "easting" three-figure reference, first. Remember the "eastings" are the **vertical lines** which run in series **across** the map.

Then give the "northing" three-figure reference. These are the **horizontal lines** which run **up** the map. Put together you have a six-figure map reference with which to locate any spot on the map that you require.

The rule then, is "eastings" before "northings". You can remember this by recalling that "E" comes before "N" in the alphabet, or by the mental reminder that when giving a map reference you go **along the corridor, then up the stairs.**

Rest assured that you will, not infrequently, both give and receive incorrect map references, where the eastings and northings have been reversed. It is a common error, so look out for it. Also remember that you give **all** the eastings before the northings. Do **not** give the grid square numbers and then follow it with the two grid reference numbers. For example, in Fig. 1 the tumulus is at **914414**, not at **914144**. See the difference? Try exchanging a few map references with your wife, children or a friend. You will soon get the hang of it.

Now for a few examples, using Fig. 1.
1. What lies at 925425?
2. If you are at 902418, where are you?
3. What lies at 900389?
4. What sort of road runs from 898422 to 917429?
5. What lies at 916429?
The answers are:
1. Church with tower.
2. You are at a church—what sort of church? One with a spire.
3. A cross roads.
4. A second class metalled road.

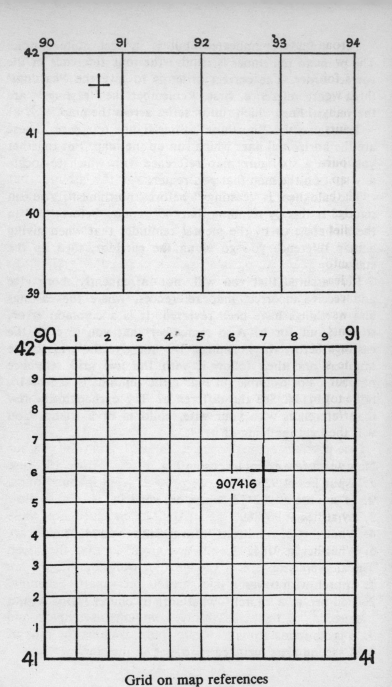

Grid on map references

5. A road bridge over a railway line.

Now take the answers, and work out the map references for yourself. See if they agree with those given here. Then work out plenty of others until you can do it easily.

Finally, before going out on the ground, let us look at **contours**.

Contours

A map is a pictorial representation of the ground, but while the map is flat, the ground is bumpy; not to mention rolling, hilly or mountainous. These changes in the level, or **relief** of the land are indicated on O.S. maps by contour lines.

Contours are quite easy to follow, provided you grasp the idea that a contour is an imaginary line following the surface of the ground at a specific level. The contour follows the same height, round the hills, into the re-entrants, and over the spurs. Contours make no effort to indicate the relief, but they can give you a very good idea of the shape of the land. On the 1:50,000 O.S. map the contour lines are 50 feet apart. Therefore, if the lines are close together it follows that the land is rising very quickly. If far apart, that the slope is gentle. If at irregular intervals that the land undulates.

One point that foxes people is to know from the contour lines whether the land is rising or falling, whether a feature is a spur or re-entrant. A spur projects from the land mass, while a re-entrant is exactly the opposite i.e., a shallow valley reaching into the mass. Apart from experience, these points will help. Firstly, the contour values, which are given to the nearest metre, are given so that they read facing uphill. Remember though that while the heights are in metres, the contour lines are 50 feet apart. Secondly, you can compare the contour values which are given at regular intervals along the line. Thirdly, commonsense. Rivers and streams do not normally run up spurs or along the tops of hills. Often other features will give you the clue.

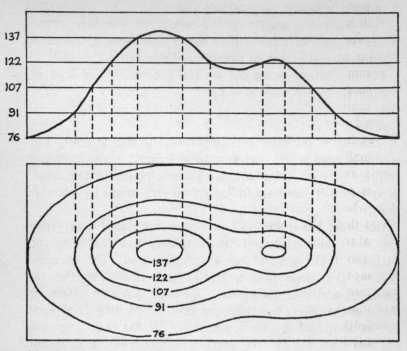

CONTOURS OF A HILL WITH A COL

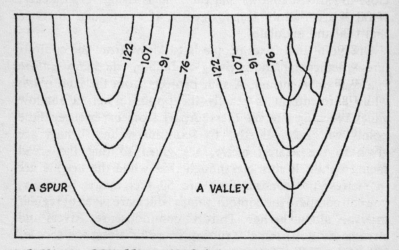

A SPUR   A VALLEY

DIFFERENCE BETWEEN A SPUR AND A VALLEY OR RE-ENTRANT

Contour lines

Apart from contours, height is indicated by **spot heights** which are indicated on the map as follows: • 117. This is the precise height, in metres, above sea level at this particular point. You will also find **trig points,** indicated on the map as follows: Δ 180. This again is the exact height above sea level, and on the spot you will find a concrete triangular obelisk with metal fittings in the top. This supported surveying instruments when the map was made. There is one on the map facing page 21 at M.R. 938389.

Finally, apart from contour lines, very steep slopes or cliffs are shown by a visual reproduction of a cliff, or a series of sharp jagged arrowheads. Be wary of areas like this when out on the ground.

At this point you are ready to go out of doors for some visual map reading. You will not yet need a compass.

Study your local map and find a spot, on a local hill perhaps, which seems to offer good visibility over the surrounding landscape. Go there and sit down, with the map unfolded before you. The first task is to "set" or "orient" the map.

This means, quite simply, turning the map until it coincides with the ground before you. This may mean that the map is sideways, or upside down, to you. Don't worry. You can still read it like that, and it means that objects on the ground, which can't move, will appear in the correct place and where you expect them. Many people go wrong when map reading because they hold the map like a book, the right reading way up, and turn left when they should turn right, or spend hours looking in the wrong direction for landmarks. Get the map **set** on your position and, as you move, keep it that way. You can always turn it the right way up for a quick peek, to read a name. Otherwise keep it aligned to the ground.

With the map **set** or **oriented**, fix your position accurately by visual checks. Note that at this stage we are not asking you to use a compass or compass bearings, only to read a map.

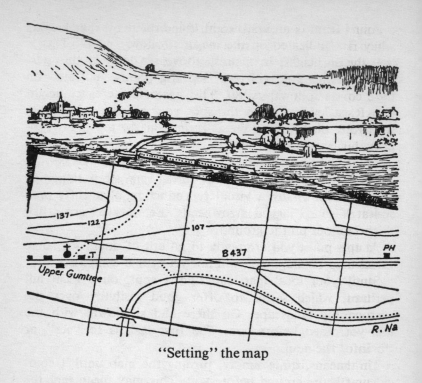

"Setting" the map

Now, let us go on a brief imaginary map march, using the map illustration, Fig. 1.

FIGURE 1: Our position is the road junction at Tytherington, M.R. 916411. This is easy to fix as, apart from being the road junction, there is a church without tower or steeple there, probably a chapel. Our object is to walk south-east towards Whatcomb Bottom.

Our first task is to orient the map, by turning it on its side thus placing Whatcombe Bottom in the top right-hand corner.

We can now pick a route, first down the road ahead of us for about 400 metres/yards. 400 metres = 430 yards approximately. One metre is roughly 39 inches.

We will pass óne track on our right, then a building on our left, then we take the next road right. Notice the contour lines. As we walk south (turn the map) the land is slowly rising. We come to a track junction and bear left, (turn the map). We have the land rising quite steeply now on our right-hand side. It rises about 40 feet.

We continue along the track until we come to a building at M.R. 921403, where the track turns sharply right. We could follow the track, which is rising ahead of us up the slope, but let us strike out across the fields towards the minor road that runs between M.R. 926407 and Corton Down. If this was a long distance, a compass would be necessary, but it is not far and there is a building on the road at M.R. 927401, which will act as a check. On reaching the road we turn right and walk down, with the land rising up on our right, note spot height 117 metres, until we reach the track on the left, M.R. 926393. We go down this until it bears sharply left again. At this point there is a **re-entrant** facing us—see the contours—and we walk into the re-entrant to arrive at Whatcombe Bottom.

As you can see from this example, the map is stuffed with information that makes it easy to move from spot to spot in the required direction.

Your task now is to go on a short map march, in your own area, off roads where possible, and, fixing your position as you go, try judging from the map what you will find ahead **before** you get there. This will quickly build up your skill and, equally important, your confidence.

If, on your walk, you come upon a hill, or some spot with a good view, stop and spend time finding and identifying landmarks from ground to map and map to ground.

Calculate distances, and remember to keep the map "set". A pair of 8 x 30 field glasses can be useful.

Constant comparison of map and ground, and keeping the map "set", will quickly give you the ability to read a map. Now, let us learn how to work with a compass.

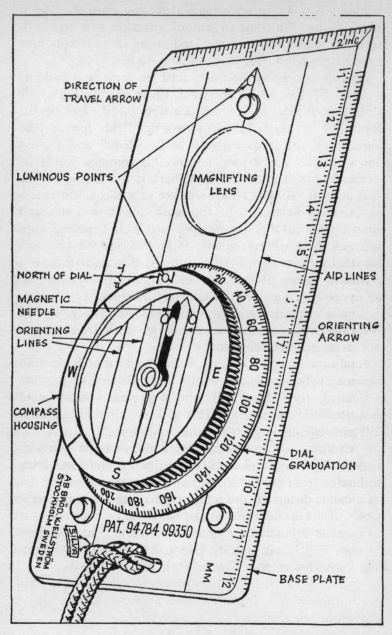

The Silva Compass

4

Compass Work

For this section we are assuming the possession and use of the Silva compass. There are other models available, and many people are still familiar with the heavy military prismatic compass, used in conjunction with a protractor. With the Silva, the protractor is unnecessary, and the compass is widely available, not expensive, and simple to use.

Study the diagram opposite and note the names of the various parts.

Even without a map, a compass is useful. It can enable you to walk in a straight line, and head in a general direction, so that if, for example, you forgot the map, or took the wrong one, and only found out your error when life got sticky, a compass can be very useful. Wandering around in circles until you collapse from exhaustion is one fate you can probably avoid, especially if you can remember the main features from the map, and know roughly where you are. This situation ought not to arise, but if it does, TRUST THE COMPASS. Don't feel it must be wrong and go your own way. TRUST THE COMPASS.

Map and compass are complementary. You need both a compass **and** a map and you need to know how to use them.

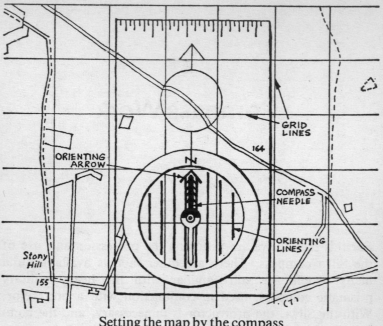

Setting the map by the compass

Setting the Map by the Compass

You have already learned to **orient** or **set** the map by aligning it to features on the ground. You can also set the map with the compass.

This is a useful skill if you are in the mountains, hills, or on a featureless plain. You need to know where North lies in order to 'set' a map. First set the magnetic variation on the compass. Then place the compass on the map with the compass needle to north and turn the **map** until the orienting lines (on the compass) lie parallel to the **grid** lines (on the map). Now you know which way you are facing, the direction of North, and can start to try and identify points on the ground from the map, or vice-versa.

Finding Your Position by Compass:
Converting Compass Bearings to Grid Bearings

To find your position you need two or more identifiable features or **landmarks** on the ground, that you can also find on the map. These should preferably be some distance apart, at right-angles to each other, so that you have cross-bearings to fix your position. This is called 're-section'.

You may know where your landmarks are on the map and ground, but you don't know where you are. To find out, take the following action.

Take the Silva compass in the left hand and point the Travel arrow directly at the landmark. Then, holding the compass steady, swivel the compass housing until the needle

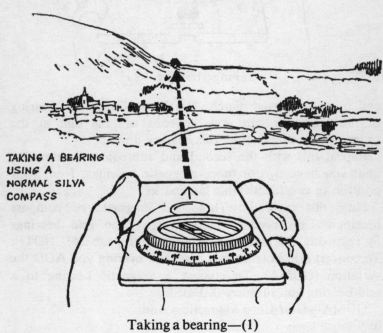

TAKING A BEARING
USING A
NORMAL SILVA
COMPASS

Taking a bearing—(1)

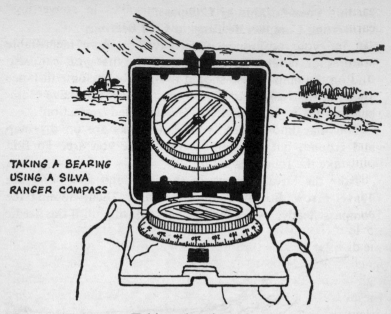

TAKING A BEARING
USING A SILVA
RANGER COMPASS

Taking a bearing—2

and orienting arrow match, North to North. The bearing of the landmark can now be read off the dial at the Index pointer mark. Note this bearing down.

Repeat this with the second and subsequent landmarks, until you have two or more **magnetic** bearings, from your position to two identifiable landmarks.

Note this carefully: These are **magnetic** or compass bearings. They need to be converted into **grid bearings** by removing the **magnetic variation** (see page 35). NOTE: To convert **grid bearing** to a magnetic **bearing** you ADD the variation (GUMA). To convert a **magnetic bearing** to a grid bearing you subtract (MUGS).

GUMA—**G**rid **U**nto **M**agnetic = **A**dd

or

MUGS—**M**agnetic **U**nto **G**rid = **S**ubtract

The mnemonic GUMA or MUGS, from the first letter of each word, is one way of remembering what to do to convert bearings. People frequently make mistakes in converting bearings, and this may help you get it right.

In the present case we have to **subtract** the magnetic variation from the magnetic bearing, to get a grid bearing. So, if our magnetic bearings were 300° and 50° respectively and the magnetic variation was 8°, our grid bearings would be 292° and 42° respectively.

These are the bearings from your position to the landmarks, from a point you cannot identify to two (or more) points you can. You can find your position as follows:

Set the first magnetic bearing on the dial of the compass, and then deduct the variation. This automatically gives you the grid bearing. Forget the compass bearing, you no longer need it. Place the compass on the map. Place the direction line over the first landmark, with the landmark as close to the compass dial as possible. Then, keeping the sighting line over the landmark, swivel the compass until the **orienting lines** are parallel with the **grid lines**, with the orienting arrow pointing north. Next, at the point where the sighting line runs off the compass, mark the map with a dot, making a map mark.

Now, using the edge of the compass as a ruler, draw a pencil line connecting the map mark and the landmark, and run it back towards you. Your position is somewhere along that line.

Repeat the process on the second landmark. The line from this point should cut the first line, and where they cut, you are.

Remember the steps:
1. Identify two or more landmarks on the ground and on the map.
2. Take magnetic bearings.
3. Deduct the magnetic variation to make a grid bearing.
4. Set these bearings on the compass and draw in a series of intersecting lines on the map.
5. Where the lines intersect is your position.

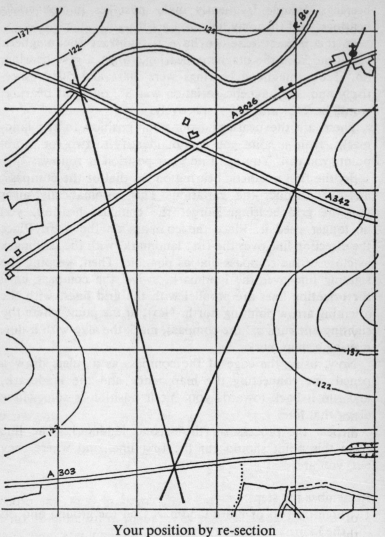

Your position by re-section

Now, so far we have used the compass to set the map, and to find your position.

The same process can be used to march between two points. This may seem irrelevant, for, when you can see your landmark or object, why do you need a compass bearing to reach it? However, if you wanted to reach it through a thick wood, in fog, or at night, then a compass bearing to march on would be invaluable.

Grid Bearings into Magnetic or
Compass Bearings

To obtain a grid bearing, you have first to identify your position, and your objective on the map.

Lay the edge of the compass down as a line to connect these two points, then turn the compass housing until the orienting lines are parallel to the grid lines. Ignore the compass needle at this point.

You can now read off the grid bearing at the index pointer. Remember this is a grid bearing, and to convert it into a magnetic or compass bearing, you have to ADD the magnetic variation i.e., grid unto magnetic add, or **GUMA**.

Let us say that the magnetic variation is again 8°, so if your grid bearing is 250, you add 8°, and set the compass dial to 258.

You can now put the map away, and, taking the compass in the left hand, simply swivel yourself around until the north point of the magnetic needle, centres over the north point of the orienting arrow. To march in the correct direction, you keep the needles together and start off, in the direction indicated by the travel arrow.

Marching on a Compass Bearing

This is the real crux of map and compass work; the process of calculating a bearing on a map, translating it on to the compass, and then, using both compass **and** map, marching to and arriving at your destination, easily, economically and safely, in all weathers, day or night.

Most of the steps will be already familiar to you, but are well worth going over once again. The steps to take are these:

37

can start to wander off line. However, if you keep the hill you started from behind you on a constant bearing of 330°, you know you are still on the right line for your objective.

You can use this technique to fix your position, by using the backbearing from an object to fix your position, or, if the backbearing cuts another point behind you, to establish your line.

Also, if you are marching on an objective, mist may obscure the objective ahead, while the point you have left is still clear.

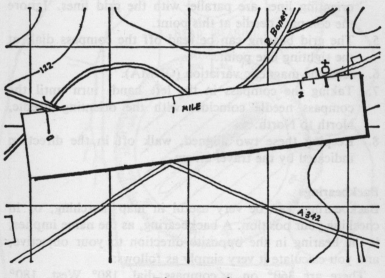

Distance scale

Distances
Distances can be calculated by marking off the distance scale from the map, on the edge of a piece of paper, and then applying it to the pencil line connecting your position with your objective.

On the 1:50,000 map, 2cm = 1 kilometre, or 1¼" = 1 mile. Each map square side is one kilometre long. This inform-ation should enable you to make some fairly accurate

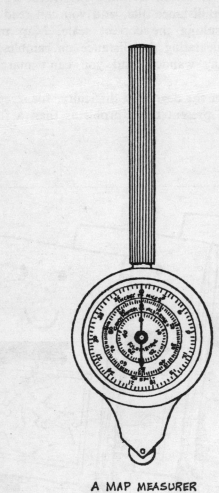

A MAP MEASURER

assessments of distance.

You can also purchase, quite cheaply, a map measure. This is a small instrument, with a distance dial in various scales, and a travel wheel. Running the travel wheel over the map turns the distance dial, and you can read off the distance by consulting the correct scale. Map measures are useful for calculating the distance on rambles, where the footpaths may wander, and you can't march in a straight line.

Finally, consider the degree of difficulty, for steep slopes or woodland will present more problems than a flat level plain.

Maps Marching!!

5

Map Marching

Hints on Map Marching

Experience is the best, indeed, almost the only teacher. There is no substitute for practical work, with map and compass on the ground. However, the following tips, if you have the wit to use them, may prove helpful.

1. **Distance:** You can calculate the distance of your march from the map, but on the ground it will probably be further. Certain obstacles block your path and some diversion is inevitable. So if you calculate a walk of say six miles, be prepared for it to be nearer eight, by the time you have finished.

2. **Time:** Realise the effect that this will have on time. Not only will you walk further, it will take longer. How fast can you walk? Most people, reasonably fit, can average about four miles per hour on roads or pavement. Once off this, on to tracks and footpaths, the speed drops dramatically, and if you have to keep stopping to consult map and compass, it can drop further still. Time, inevitably, is a factor. Night may be arriving, mist closing in, train or bus to catch. Always allow more time than you need. You'll need it.

3. **Use the Map and Compass Regularly:** Always know where you are. Regularly check your position. This may not matter so much in southern suburban England,

but on the moors or mountains, mist or cloud can close in with startling speed. Within minutes you can have visibility of a few metres. Provided you know where you are, and have a few bearings, there is nothing to worry about.

4. **Trust the Compass:** You may think you know best, and that it must be wrong. Inevitably, if you do so, and head off in the direction your sense of direction tells you is the right one, you will get gloriously lost, and the complications can be unpleasant.

5. **Practice:** Practice map and compass marching at night or in fog. The problems are the same. You can easily practice night or fog marching on a winter's evening, by doing a compass march around the local park or common. Don't wait till you are up a mountain to discover your limitations.

6. **Beware of Magnetic Attraction:** Put a knife by the Silva compass and watch the needle veer. The needle is affected by metal, by wire, fences and gates, telegraph

Beware of magnetic attraction

wires, metal plates, even a metal propelling pencil. Don't work out bearings on the bonnet of the car, and, if you can, keep well away from metal objects of any kind while taking a bearing.

7. **Don't expect to compass march to your objective with pin-point accuracy.** An error of 5° either side of your line of march is to be expected. In daylight, using the map as well, you can be very accurate indeed, but at night, or in fog or close country, it is better to pick a landmark you can't possibly miss, a road or a river say, or a large plantation, and march on that. You can take bearings to establish your exact position when you arrive in the general area of your objective. The time you save by not creeping along with your head in the map, or over the compass, striving for unattainable pin-point accuracy, can be used here. You will also enjoy your walk much more if you take a look at the scenery.

8. **Marching at Night or in Fog:** At night or in fog, except for very large visible landmarks, or unless it is a clear, bright, night, you will need to use the compass. Get out your Silva compass now, and study it again. Various points on it are luminous, notably the North point of the needle and the area on the compass dial around the sight line. The sight line, and the orienting arrow are picked out with luminous dots. Setting the compass in the normal way, you can use these luminous marks to keep it aligned while marching. Do not use a torch at night if you can help it. It destroys your night vision temporarily.

9. **Pacing at night:** Distance is difficult to calculate and it may be necessary to pace out the bounds or **legs** of your trip. Roughly 150 paces at night is 100 metres. This is very rough, and depends on your height, the difficulty of the ground, and your confidence in taking a decent stride. Try pacing distances when practising map marching at night in the local park, and see what

45

the pace: distance ratio is for you. Another useful tip, if you are in a group and in difficult country, is to take it in turns to pace out the distance. The average of the group will be pretty constant, and can prove surprisingly accurate.

10. **If you start going wrong:** Or you think you are going wrong, stop and re-calculate your position. Once errors start they tend to multiply, and you can fool yourself into believing that one hill **must** be the one you want even when other landmarks indicate that it isn't. You can march miles in the wrong direction like this. If in doubt, stop and check. If possible, always get your partner to re-check your calculations or do his own as well, and then make a comparison.

Route Cards

For most map marches you will not be able to proceed from A to B in a straight line. Almost inevitably you will have to march in a series of legs, to get round a river, reach a bridge, avoid a swamp or some such obstacle.

It will save much time and trouble if you prepare your route in advance by noting the legs on a **route card**.

You can draw these up easily for yourself, and note down as much information as necessary, but a typical route card looks like this:

Sheet no: 184: Start: Farm 896401 Finish: Hill 912442 Mag variation: 8°

Start	Mag°	Finish	Distance	Time
896401	88°	Barn 909403	2Km	45 mins
909403	48°	Church 916411	1Km (by track)	20 mins
916411	Map	Church 925424	3Km.Rd./F.pth	45 mins
925424	Map	Tumulus 920432	1Km-uphill	30 mins
920432	326°	Hill 912442	1Km	20 mins
	TOTAL	DISTANCE	8Km (5 miles)	160 mins 2 hrs. 40 mins say: 3 hrs.

Preparing a route card is the ideal way for youth clubs or rambling groups to set out map reading problems or ramble instructions.

People can walk the route in various ways and it provides the walkers with all the necessary information, and by setting it out in this way, forces them to consider problems of time, distance and difficulty of terrain. To walk the route in the opposite direction you convert the given bearings into backbearings, and otherwise just use the map.

Obstacle Crossing

Moving across county it is inevitable that even in farming country, you will encounter obstacles that cannot be crossed, and must be circumvented. The problem is to do this without losing direction.

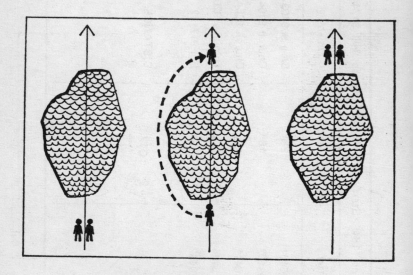

Obstacle crossing by bearings—1

Basically, if you can see across the obstacle, a small lake say, then there is no real problem. You take a bearing in some prominent point on the far side, and then go around the lake until you reach it. You can also take a back-bearing from where you are, and walk round the lake until you pick up the bearing again, behind your first position.

If there is no prominent object on either side, one member of the party can be sent round to mark the bearing, and stay on the line until the rest catch up.

If you **cannot** see over or through the obstacle, a thick wood say, or an estuary, then you will have no option but to go round the obstacle in a series of right angled legs, pacing out each leg, to be roughly certain when you come back on line. The diagram below sets this procedure out clearly.

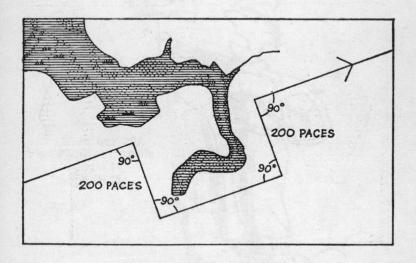

Obstacle crossing by bearings—2

6

Planning Your Map March

If you have worked your way steadily through this book,
done all the exercises, and been out in the country with
map and compass, you should, by now, have a pretty
fair idea of what you are doing, and feel confident in
your ability to find your way about. You will probably
also have made a few mistakes, and be ready for some
more instruction. There is a lot of truth in the saying that
you only learn by mistakes. A mistake once made, then
sorted out, and solved, sticks in the mind far better than
any amount of academic study.

Moreover, mistakes make one more willing to heed advice.
At this stage, mistakes are made, not so much through
lack of knowledge, as through lack of organization.

Let us assume that you feel confident enough to use
your map and compass skills in fairly rough country, and
are planning a map march across the Welsh Mountains
from Bangor.

Before you set off, the three in the party—and there
should be **at least** three in case of unforeseen accidents,
or injury—need to get organized. We will deal here with
the organization of the route finding.

Can you answer 'yes' to the following questions:—
1. Do you have all the maps necessary to cover the
    route?

2. Are they up to date?
3. Do you know the magnetic variation?
4. Have you a compass?
5. Is it functioning correctly?
6. Have you calculated the "legs" of your route?
7. Have you prepared a route card?
8. Has one of your companions also prepared a route card?
9. Do they agree?
10. Has the third member checked the calculations?
11. Have you allowed enough time?
12. Have you got full notes, sharp pencils, map case, roamers and all other necessary equipment?

If you can answer a definite "yes" to all these questions, you can pack up your equipment and set off with an easy mind, knowing that you will not need to huddle under a rock in the rain, and waste time, working out your route, when you arrive at the starting point.

Checking Your Compass
Modern compasses, like the Silva, are precision made, and can stand up to a great deal of hard treatment. Needless to say, they should be carefully looked after, and kept in a safe place. If the luminous spots get chipped, you can touch them up with a dab of luminous paint and if you even suspect that a night march will ever be necessary, be sure that the luminous spots are in good order.

It is a common curse of map marching to feel that the compass is wrong. You may be right, up to a point, if the compass is being deflected by a rucksack full of metal equipment, but from time to time, if only to put your mind at rest, you can check your compass for accuracy by either:
1. Comparing the readings with another compass.
2. Comparing the compass with known North points, and checking that the needle points accurately in that direction.

3. Comparing the compass with the weathercock direction on church steeples.

7

Alternative Route Finding

We have already explained that map marching is more of an art than exact science. You can be very accurate indeed, if you use map and compass together, and correctly, but, not infrequently, you will not care very much **exactly** where you are going, as long as it is in the correct general direction.

You can, for interest's sake, put your map and compass away, and try some other methods of general route finding.

1. The Sun:

The sun rises in the East and sinks in the West. In the U.K. and the northern hemisphere generally, the sun travels through the southern sky, so that such shadow as is cast at mid-day will point North. Even without this, if you know which is West and East, you will know North. Some people have difficulty in remembering which lies on which side, so if you remember that the West and East initial letters make up the word WE, this will help to avoid confusion.

2. Use your watch:

You can use the hand on the watch to indicate **South**. Lay the watch on the palm of your hand with the hour hand pointing at the sun. True South (not magnetic) will be midway between the hour hand and 12 o'clock. Remember to allow for Summer-time, if applicable, and put the hands back to Greenwich time.

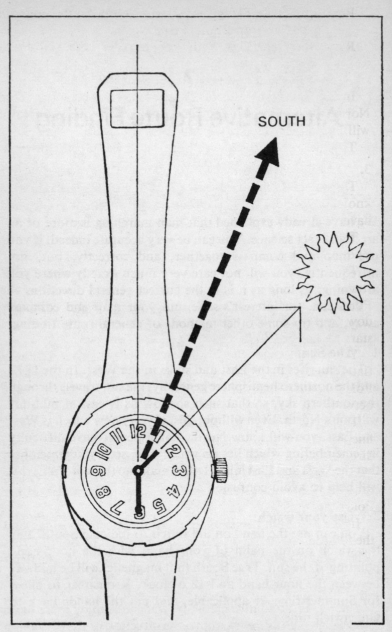

North by sun and wrist-watch

Remember: i This gives you true South. So the opposite direction is true North.

Remember: ii This only applies in the Northern hemisphere.

iii You need to see the sun.

In the Southern hemisphere, the rules are reversed. True North is found by pointing 12 o'clock at the sun, and North will be between 12 o'clock and the hour hand.

This method is not very accurate, but is well worth knowing.

3.   True North by the Stars

This is something that every outdoor enthusiast ought to know. On a clear night the stars are an excellent guide, and have been used by marine navigators for centuries.

The position of The Pole Star is found by lining up the **"pointer"** stars on the Plough, or Great Bear.

This group is easily found, as it consists of seven bright stars in a clear group. All the stars in it revolve around the Pole Star and can lie in any position, left, right, or upside down, relative to the Pole Star. The two, end, or "pointer" stars will always indicate the Pole Star however.

You can also use the other group of stars, shaped like a flat W, called Cassiopeia. It lies on the opposite side of the Pole Star from the Plough. The Pole Star lies about midway between the two groups.

The Pole Star lies exactly North, where it lies exactly in line, above or below, with the two "pointers". Or it lies directly above a point half-way behind the two stars which make the left-hand arm of the W of Cassiopeia. Study the drawings on the next page, and go out tonight and find the Pole Star.

In the Southern hemisphere, the Pole Star is invisible, and the South Cross is used to find true South. The South Cross is less useful than the North Star, and is both more difficult to calculate with, and less accurate. See the diagram for directions.

Finally, as alternative methods, you can employ more basic knowledge such as, for example, the direction of the prevailing

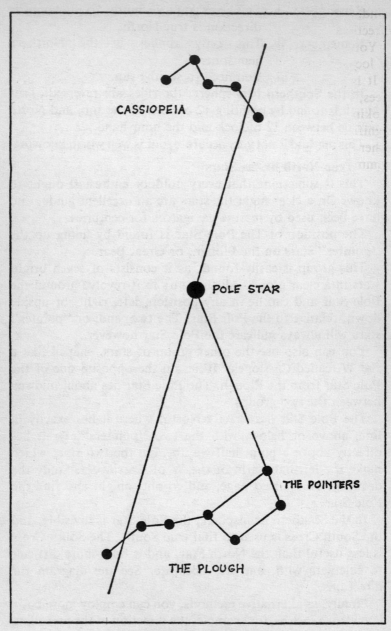

CASSIOPEIA

POLE STAR

THE POINTERS

THE PLOUGH

Finding the Pole Star

wind, which can bend trees permanently in the opposite direction.

You can remember the watershed, and study the direction of local streams.

It is said that moss grows thicker on the North side of trees, and no doubt this is true. However, half a lifetime looking for this useful phenomena has failed to show us any significant difference between the north side of trees and any other side. Perhaps it is best to stick to map, compass, and common sense, after all.

IT'S EITHER A CHURCH
WITH A SPIRE —
OR A GIANT'S ORB.

8

Further Training

As we explained in the beginning, you can only learn the rudiments of map reading from a book. It is a skill, and like all skills, is only acquired and developed by regular practice.

The curious thing about map marching is that it is also something of an art. Some people just never seem to get lost, can move across country at their desired speed, and come out just where they intended. Those who plod nervously across the moors, never able to make the ground and map match, and come out five miles west of where they want to, find this ability in others both baffling, and a mite depressing.

The secret, such as it is, lies in organization, routine, good training, and above all, confidence. Combine all this with lots of practice and, like Eliza Doolittle, by Jove you'll get it!

Further training then must take the form of practice, practice and more practice.

A good way to develop skill is to pass your knowledge on to others. Fellow campers or ramblers, your wife and family, will all be the better for a bit of instruction and in preparing to instruct others, you will clarify problems for yourself.

It only remains, therefore, for us to wish you good luck and good fun, in your future out of doors, and hope that your way will be obvious, and your errors infrequent!